the broom tree

Poems

Gregory Ramkawsky

the broom tree
Copyright © 2023 Gregory Ramkawsky
Published by Unsolicited Press.
Printed in the United States of America.
First Edition.

No part of this book may be used or reproduced in any manner whatsoever without written permission except in the case of brief quotations embodied in critical articles or reviews.

Attention schools and businesses: for discounted copies on large orders, please contact the publisher directly.

For information contact:
Unsolicited Press
Portland, Oregon
www.unsolicitedpress.com
orders@unsolicitedpress.com
619-354-8005

Cover Designer: Kathryn Gerhardt
Editor: S.R. Stewart and Kristen Marckmann

ISBN: 978-1-956692-82-2

Poems

One: Ipesity

Nosce Te Ipsum	2
On Robert Siegel's Retirement	5
Maybe	7
In Progress	8
A Prayer: Part I	11
Spiral	15
Constitution	18
Moraino	19
Barely Literate	21
Liquid to be Concerned With	24
Landscape	25
Anagrams	26

Two: Interlude

Axon Transit	30
Torpor	31
A Prayer: Part II	32
14	35
5/9/18	36
Silence	37
Service Elevator	38

   Escape as an Open Window   39
   Chrysalis   40

Three: I Am
   Tuck Me In   43
   Simultaneous   45
   Cold   47
   Christopher Wren's Tombstone   48
   Forget Me   49
   Black Holes   51
   Hemingway, Neruda, Chopin, and the Baptist   54
   Something Less Than What We Are   55
   On Attending a Writing Workshop   57
   On Attending a Writing Workshop Redux   60
   Struggle   63
   A Prayer: Part III   68
   The Scribe and the Prophet   71
   Beyond Beersheba   72

Afterward: 74
Benediction   76
Notes   78

For my wife, Tamsen

One:

Ipseity

"I'm just not who I thought I'd be."
—From "Freefall (From Hand to Hand)" by Stavesacre

Nosce Te Ipsum[1]

If you want to know me,
Curate me, slow and quiet,
Digest as the alimentary canal,
Learn, absorb, assimilate
Rifle through my collected
Objects, memory chains of paper
Boxed obscurely, tied loosely,
Pressed or framed or anonymously
Rolled as a grave stone,   find
An epitaph to carve, encapsulated
Statement tied errant strands,
Items savored as a song lyric
Connected invisibly like gravity
Maintaining feet upon the mountains.

If you want to know me,
Hear me, slow and quiet,
Desire as a marriage bed,
Listen to yarn unspun
From sweaters, scarves,   attending
To the warmth and covering,
Complementing an otherwise
Unremarkable and steady pace,
Water like voices clamoring
As waves blown, crashing,

---

[1] Latin meaning "Know Thyself"

And broom tree's shadow whispers
Testifying to matters greater
As we apprehend each other
Through the witching.

If you want to know me,
Read me, slow and quiet,
Deep as a waterfall basin,
Parse the locution written, left
Behind to period testimony,
Pierce the misty sheets, the wake
Rustling, searching the hearts of
Those who search for me,
Symbolized as Ozymandias,
King of Kings, behold what
King reigns, what rocks
Pepper the plunge pool,   what
Moss grows scaly as a basilisk
Running 'cross the veiled waters.

If you want to know me,
Kill me, slow and quiet,
Deliberate as a hummingbird,
Look into my eyes, windows
Through which my soul escapes
See beyond the pain to pain's   response,
Dig past the outward phrases
Unearth the fuel of treasures buried deep,
Furnace them to knifely fire,
Glimpse the pure refinement:

Fear and hope and submission,
Sorrow and resignation and victory
Transmuted as a soaking rain,
"A concatenation of rainbows."[i]

If you want to know me,
Compile me, slow and quiet,
Disremember as the Lethe,
Pursue the records kept
By those impacted prior,
Pieced as puzzlement,
Cut from clothe containing
Elements of what's the same,
Spun with threads of what is not
Garment donned, projected
Unspun, weaved, unraveled, stitched,
Again and again, thin as old skin
As aging memory, as   happiness
"The blameless vestal's lot."[ii]

On Robert Siegel's Retirement

How odd
That his departure
Should elicit emotion
I have listened to,
All Things Considered,
For more than 10 years
And I don't know the man.
I remember, early on,
Eating French fries,
Listening to special coverage
In November '07.
My wife was pregnant
With our second child
And our daughter
Was 10 months old,
She was just starting
To put one foot
In front of the other
Without toppling over.
We lived in a duplex then
And the world,
The people in the world,
Their stories
Were starting to matter
To me.
My bubble had burst
Just a few months prior

On my first trip to India,
Where I prayed
With a leper
And he wept, then
Apologized and told me
Christ was enough,
And for three days after
I struggled
Because he knew something,
A secret
Born of suffering
That I hadn't learned.
I'm still not certain
I can learn it.

Maybe

Now we sit in the back row—now we nod at people
Politely . . . maybe we are a cemetery, maybe
We are a car crash/car crash/car crash/
Car crash/car crash/car crash/car crash, maybe
We are an empty vampire church and/or the erasure
Of it—the foundation stones of remembrance, maybe
We are a demolished craft store, an appliance dump,
The intersecting roads that lead to the same places, maybe
We are 2:30 am loneliness/starry sky/memory, maybe
We are a side street, a white-shirted spectacle, maybe
We are a wreath of dried flowers, a marker,
A monument to the dead and a memo to the living, maybe
We are a hunting camp that belongs to someone else:
Piety/hospitality/exorcism/volleyball, maybe
We are relationship in trial, in difficulty, maybe
We are a half-burned restaurant no one remembers
Or the tears that couldn't put the fire out, maybe
We are the body with a back row for people like us.

In Progress

For Makayla

They asked,
    "Why is your mom
    Always pictured sleeping?"   They asked,
        "Why do you sketch rooms
        Without any doors, forests without any
trees?"   They asked,
"Is that you with crimson?
Arms? Legs? Tears?"   They asked,
    "Is that you, alone, faceless
    Under a dark, veiled sky?"
    They asked,
"Why are you surrounded
With unbridled vulgarity?"   They observed:
    "You never draw your dad."

And she answered:
"My mother isn't sleeping,
She's passed out
    Drunk,
And I was afraid.
    I had tried for three hours
        To wake her up, but she—
        Well, she was de-stressing.

And my father left me
When I was a few years old,
        So I don't draw him
        Because I don't know him.
I am trapped in solitude,
    There is no way out
    But something must get out,
Crimson claret stains my limbs
When I open my veins
And inflict the pain
I know I deserve.
          No one has ever said
    'You are worthless,'
They didn't have to,
        I know they meant it
And it hurts so bad inside
    That my mental anguish
        Must find solace in physical agony.
I am alone
Surrounded by wilderness
        And darkness,
And no one knows
    Because I stay silent,
And everyone knows
    But they stay silent
        And watch me wander
        Whispering one to another:

'Whore, Rebel, User, Fake, Liar, Failure!

She should have been aborted!
    No one will ever love her!
        No one cares!
She should embrace apathy
    And kill herself!
        No one will remember her.'

They must be right
    When their eyes
        proclaim these things,
    When their faces
        Cloud over.
    Besides, boys seem to think
They can just take from me
And I can't stop them . . .
I was a toddler
    When I was first molested
        And my body has become
A temple for them to worship in.
    I am sacrificed on my own altar
    And I deserve it."

A Prayer: Part I

Prayer is struggle,
Dialogue,
Desperation for action
Outside free will supersession
And sovereignty, displaced
Deference of personal choice
And consequence,
Hope without guarantee,
Alleviation of pain,
Tearing out the heart
Extending, still dripping blood,
And a hole, emptied
Of fleshy imposter,
Black-dressed, spasmodic,
Laid to rest in streams,
King's hand held, directed
To crush out the wine;
A chalice, studded
With despair, longing, woundedness
Filled with the end
Misunderstood from the beginning,
Consumed confusion . . . reeling,
Drunk with iniquity, dribbling
Down the chin
Without a napkin
To wipe the dual-spring
Mouth of impurity and praise;

Intercession, fights and campaigns
On behalf of unmet expectation,
Emptying the mind; Lazarus' tomb,
Musty stench of bleached death,
Decay and empty grave clothes,
Shroud of the hidden
Beneath the revealed
Will of one who acts
Outside the realm
Of human control,
Reason, truth, morality,
And rage of nations,
Arrayed in clamor of battle,
Resisting the one
Who sits in derision,
Seeing the rage of nations
Within the sphere
Of space and time,
Traversed by wheels within wheels,
Upholding the firmament
With wings and eyes and fire,
Directing the course
And feeding fields unseen
Of flowers; sparrows
Out of work, without toil
Flighty, yet fed;
The cry of the owl
Surrounded in wilderness
Tar pits of hot, black anguish
Bubbling up from the bowels

Of what composes
The core of created world,
Serpent overthrow
Over the bank
Of Gerasene Sea;
Exchange of out-of-date fruit,
Rotten, without sustaining power
Or nutrient; display
Of the inside,
Clusters of figs
Gathered from impossible vines
Which wrap themselves, intertwined
With veins constricted,
Weakened heart-beat,
Faint flicker of light,
Blown coal, clay oven
Breath on the sticks
Of uncertainty and doubt,
Double-minded, wave-tossed
Expectation of misplaced reception,
Wedding guest needy
Without host-provided garment,
Dressed for battle,
Not like a man or woman,
Saint or servant,
Byway rags testimony
Of pods to fill the stomach
Of an ungrateful son,
Who deserves death,
And is embraced with robe,

And ring, and right to come,
Collapse
And face tomorrow, today.

Spiral

For Tyler Luzier

"Are you following Jesus this close?"
                                                    Close my eyes,
Cannot see where I am going,
                Where I came from,
Though accelerating.
                        [I am afraid of all I am,
                        I am afraid of all I am not]

  I am not
Following close, are you this Jesus?
                Jesus, stroking lambs awkwardly?
                      Perpetually sacrificed—
  I look again—
                Tilted head haloed in the rearview,
                    Gesturing with two fingers.
                                                Jesus?
            Madonna's white rosy cherub
Jesus? Are you following this close?

Close to the next lane, change,
Swerve my   mouth   for   Christ's
                          Sake sake sake forsake
(Co-pilot) No discernable separation

            Where are you, then?
                        Where am I?
                                      I am.
Are you following this close Jesus?
                    Are you close Jesus?

                                      Are you Jesus
                                      following this
                                      close?
Are you this close?
            Are you close Jesus, this following?
                                              Are
                                            you
                                            this
                                            follo
                                            wing?
Are you Jesus, this close following?
                            Are you close
                    following?

                                      This
                                      close
                                      follo
                                      wing?

    Driving me?
    Swerving?

Eyes   and fear   and art
Deteriorated, s c a t t e red
                            Accident debris and gravel

        PushedagainsttheJerseybarrier?
                                            Jesus?

This you following Jesus, are close?
            Are close? Is? What?
Image and imagine and
                    What gain? Loss
                    What loss? Gain
You are Jesus, following this close.
                                    [I cannot see.
                                    I am afraid.]

Constitution

Origami time bomb with a pull-here tab,
Inside-out umbrella in gale-force wind,
Out-of-order vending machine,
Yeshua's herald, saturnine,
Crack-in-cast bell,
Hermit crab without its shell,
Washed-up singer with a split lip,
And "Not even God can sink this ship!"[iii]
Failure on a park bench,
Discarded newspaper fence,
Timberland without a sole,
Sunlight to a sightless mole,
Vietnam tunnel in '74,
And they all float down here.
Antique traveler at Broom Tree Lodge,
Government subpoena question dodge,
Two copper coins in the offering box,
Hecate and the witches' plots,
Silas Marner with buyer's remorse,
And Winnie the Pooh trapped in gorse.
Downcast eyes in the public square,
I do not belong anywhere.

Moraino[2]

"Can that which is tasteless
Be eaten without salt?"

Unseasoned speech,
Incense incomplete.
Stacte, and Onycha,
Galbanum with
Pure frankincense,
And every prescribed
Offering profaned
By my presence,
Only good to be cast out.
Covenant of salt washout,
Goodman Brown cast about,
No guarantee exists
Within my shriveled frame.
The mineral I have lost
May be regained,
Even if I dipped myself
Into the Dead Sea
Or embraced the look-back
Pillar of remembrance,
I'm still a defeated army

---

[2] Greek word meaning to be foolish, to act foolishly; to make flat and tasteless (of salt that has lost its strength and flavor.) Found in Matthew 5:13 and Romans 1:22.

In the Valley of Salt
Belonging to the
People of Judah,
The culmination of
A shaker without a lid.

Barely Literate

On the bridge
I considered
The girl
Who teased
With her eyes
And told me
Of a stretch
Of beach
Resplendent
With light
And a salty,
Warm breeze . . .

I loved her,
But the heat
And the dryness,
The gritty sand
And shell shards
Reminded me
Of after school
Remedial reading,
Uncooperative tongue
Failing to pronounce
What I thought . . .

I thought I knew
My parents

Would understand,
Would encourage me,
And when I choked
On my words
The coldness
In their eyes
Reminded me
Of the magnetic
Alphabet letters
On the fridge
With no gold stars
To uphold . . .

And solitude,
Sweet morsel
Of avoidance
And mutual
Animosity,
Was like the cake
I could never
Bring to school
Because I have
A summer birthday . . .

My mind,
So curious,
The thrill
Of the hunt,
Looking downward
My chest heaved . . .

Like the time
Last-picked,
The kickball
Passed through
My hands,
The loss
Was bitter . . .

A mouthful
Of sea water,
Bitter . . .

A jumbled alphabet
Blank fridge,
Bitter . . .

The solitude
Of remediation,
Bitter . . .

Dispassionately
I approached
The water,
The rocks,
The decomposing
Ground swell,
I really
Misread that one.

Liquid to be Concerned With

For Christopher and Annabelle Wold

In a dream,
When my brother asks,
"Do you know what it is
To have a wound that never heals?"
I am my brother
Asking myself about pain
Beyond milky, experiential knowledge.
And when my northern battlement,
Speaking a priori, declares,
"Every savior dies."
It is the myocardial divide
Dissolving to blood,
Falling from a passing cloud.
When fingers transform
To rivers underneath,
They are ten lepers
Loudly decrying themselves
As I approach myself.
And when I am alone and unfamiliar,
I am liquid to be concerned with,
Dripping from a clay vessel,
Watering a Rose of Jericho
Until, waking, I forget.

Landscape

I
Am not
Blue mountains
Rising from the earth to meet the sky,
Not the land above the tree line
Where lichen cling to tired stone faces,
Not the dappled branches extending
In vulnerability their green, fringed fingers,
Not the amber waves in the foothills
Or the whispers before the winnowing
I am not the cultivated vineyard
Where fruit is grown deep and sweet,
Not clusters of grapes awaiting wrath,
The crushing of despair's press,
Not the water meadow teeming with life,
Songbirds singing, nesting in the underbrush,
Not the hidden beneath the revealed
Or an aesthetic covering for insecurity,
I am not a crooked body, sanguine-filled,
Or the heart that pumps it past the lookouts.
So flow by
Clean, clear
Blood,
Flow by,
Pulsing
Body of
Wilderness.

Anagrams

~~A spider~~, A diving bell, octocrept
Out of my throat for oxygen,
Motioning with its pedipalps
Before descending to the depths,
Its silk still floats among the weeds
Growing from my quiet left atrium.
    ~~As pride~~, As a vainglorious vine climbs
    Up my esophageal lattice,
    Wrapping itself around my trellis
    Like a Burmese python, constricting
    Until my neural processes fail,
    Its shed skin hangs like a boa.
        ~~Aspired~~ As the Prince of Tyre,
        Dwelling in the heart of the sea,
        A god in my killer's company,
        Babylon's thirteen-year siege
        Like herons spearing fish in the shallows,
        While my thoughts scuttle like crabs.
~~I spread~~ My arms, wide as a net
Cast to reproach from the port,
Seabirds dive to the trough,
Stealing the cast away portions,
Eating lost hope like rotting bait
While I try to ensnare competency.

~~I parsed~~ "*Ya'ash*[3]," then, "*Exaporeomai*[4],"
I was heavy with sickness, laden
As a dream with emotion,
Utterly at a loss, resourceless
As a South Indian leper colony,
Dragging themselves limbless to supper.
                        ~~I spared~~ My family, the loss
                        Yielding to the colorful hills
                        I fell down as a Carobtree pod
                        And waited for the poor to come,
                        Like an Israeli beach soup kitchen
                        Ladled out Eritrean refugees.
                        ~~Despair~~: Hidden jewel of *Charis*
On the faces of the migrant poor,
On the faces of the lepers,
On my feckless, fearful face
Drifting in the deep spaces
Below the curtains of the world.

---

[3] Ya'ash – Hebrew word meaning to despair, to be desperate, it is hopeless

[4] Exaporeomai – Greek word meaning to be utterly at a loss, destitute of measures or resources, renounce all hope, be in despair

Two:

Interlude

"O Wedding-Guest! This soul hath been
Alone on a wide, wide sea:
So lonely 'twas, that God himself
Scarce seeméd there to be."
—From, "The Rime of the Ancient Mariner" by Samuel Taylor Coleridge

"For a minute the sky pours into the hole like plasma.
There is no hope, it is given up."
—From, "Berck-Plage" by Sylvia Plath

Axon Transit

Cinereal trees,
Ice-laden, bare
Branches gesture
In all directions.

Lost-labyrinth
Sere walls of
Impassible doubt
And winter.

Peregrinating
Axon transit—
The fog of failure—
Plagiarized feeling.

Shining Torrance
Or the too much
With us world
On the mountaintop.

Steel sky feels
As close as disquiet,
As cold as disaffection,
As silent as God.

Torpor

When lean times of famine are about,
And no word, no habitation can retain
The warmth or glow of life within the vein,
For those neither dispassionate nor devout,
They gather their belongings and go out;
Deep down beneath their common plane,
And, not noticing their common pain,
Into the torpor of their common doubt.

The lumbering and overladen bear,
Plods into the den to rest awhile,
Uncertain of what future God will bring,
Esther Greenwood, but not given to despair,
Not suicide, but truth to reconcile…
Awaiting the return of life or spring.

A Prayer: Part II

Prayer is sentiment
Succinctly stated
By a person from a pulpit
Placed as a dais above a hall
Perhaps half-filled with patrons,
Half-expecting generic blessing
Pronounced with hands spread
As protective wings
Over half-hearted congregation,
Eloquent soliloquy addressed
To generic god, presiding
Over liturgy
With countenance lifted up,
Like bronzed serpent
In the wilderness
Awaiting faithful glance,
Gaze, fixated eye
Upon the gleaming object
Representing their only hope
Of healing,
While the dead fall
Like Jericho walls!
Day Star, Son of Dawn
Whispered, blunted edge
Which cannot pierce
The veil of those
Whose ears have not

Been dug for them,
Waiting with more anticipation
For the "Amen"
Then for the passion;
Compassionate words, devoid
Of power, predictable diction,
Line upon line precepts
Hear a little, there a little musings
To anoint hidden wounds;
Expired balm of Gilead
From a squeezed-out tube,
Black robe dressed
Adorned with collar,
White robe dressed
With ornate, ornamental praise
That honors the one
Who utters them,
Learned, but never arriving
Traditionalist, traveling
Over seas and lands,
Two times child-of-Hell
Proselytes with full stomachs,
Suckled on the warm milk
Of modernity and Pharisaism,
Exalting the god
Of their invention;
Prescription medication
Creating opioid epidemic
Without clear solution,
Clear conscience Narcan distribution,

Scrubbing bubbles
Of ad hoc chemical life support,
Three times in a day
Relapse; E.R. reject,
Short-term solution
To a long-term problem
Of someone else's words
Representing their belief
Not shared,
Not owned,
Not comprehended,
Inappropriately appropriated
Forgiveness, devoid of faith
And never-enough
Casual intercession
Misdirected to the saints;
No more than words
Above the doorposts of Heaven.

14

    Anxiety imprints
      Identity
    Like fingernails
      Digging for solace
    Unearthing
      Trauma
    Hands
      Still shaking

5/9/18

finally settled out//of court amendable//we parted ways
amicably//terms clear my
heart
stopped
beating

Silence

Eyes synched shut,
Shining sun at zenith,

Dead words decomposing
In throat's grave,

Dolorous bells tolling
In heart's sepulcher,

Presupposition whispering
To itself about itself,

Exchanged glances between
Six coffin-bearers,

Snow caught in eyelashes
Of lacrimal welling,

Saying goodbye to one
Who cannot be told goodbye,

Chrysanthemums blooming
In a spring that never comes

Service Elevator

Service elevator,
A sign reads:
Closed for maintenance.

Disregarded,
Legs traverse
The chained entrance.

Familiar fingers
Depress prosaic buttons,
But no response.

A lift operator,
Determined, but
Without poetic license.

"I can't understand."
Overly simplistic
Verse about trespasses.

Upon exiting,
The bell dings
And the door closes.

Bottom floor life,
Out of service
Until further notice.

Escape as an Open Window

Ekphrastic on Young Woman at a Window[iv]

Longing as the sound of the sea
Swelling and cresting cadence,
Waves lapping at the shoreline.
Possibilities, fleeting as sand,
Swirl in and out across intertidal
Heart, grief-encrusted, shell-rimmed,
Self-determined as a tiller
Succumbing as a sailboat
To all that inescapable breath
Exhaled across life's mantle

Chrysalis

Thyroxine trigger,
  Why so proud?
Areyounotinlovewithchange?

Metamorphosis,
  An inescapable process,
Cracked cocoon
    Emergent.

Pump blood into your wings,
  Fly humbly

Lifeincrisislifeinstasis,
Extended metaphor,
  You have no voice!
(Just in time)

Three:

I Am

"We died, and we go on dying.
So where would I look for us except
In everything I see."
—From "First World" by Li-Young Lee

"It's irresponsible to despair.
And so I am hysterical enough for now."
—From "Hysteria" by Lee Upton

"Dig a hood hole!//Lay me nostrils up//and shovel in my mouth the decent black earth."
—From "Pursued by the Men of Vasenka" by Ilya Kaminsky

"I know the voices dying with a dying fall"
—From "The Love Song of J. Alfred Prufrock" by T.S. Eliot

"Most of us live out a determined forgetfulness of fight and flight. We flee from memory in fear of what the past may tell us, and then in fury fight to recreate an unencumbered present that cuts the cords to our past. This foundationless reconstruction is doomed to fail, however, because it makes us the creator of our story rather than allowing the true creator of the universe to shape our story."
—From *Forgetting to Remember* by Allender and Hudson

Tuck Me In

The earth down here
Feels warm and damp,
My clothes are soiled,
I lay down my head.
  I remember fighting,
  Struggling to stay out
  Of this human-sized hole.
I did not build a basket
Or pine box to lower
Past earth worms and beetles
To clay and old silty soil
Where it stays warm,
    And dark,
    And deep,
    And alone.
I did not clothe myself
With burlap sacking,
  With coarseness,
    With presupposition,
      With penitence.

I am just a union of dust
  With dust,

A fulfillment of the old guarantee,
That comforting return
To a better life,

                Perhaps.
The sky seems so dark
From where I lie,
      Then   a star wanders
Across my vision
(Though stars cannot "wander"
As if they were vagabonds
Traversing the skyscape
In search of trembling eyes
To lend hope to
When it's dark,
         And deep,
                    And alone)
And I am pinned
By the obvious truth,

If I dug my own grave
Who will courteously
                Tuck me in?

Simultaneous

For Zachary Madziarz

Wanting to die
Is simultaneous.

A badge of honor
Giving entrance
Into the current
Trendy elite
Self-diagnosed depression.

A banner; a flying flag,
Night has fallen,
There is blood,
Drop, drop, drop,
Of self-discovery and pain.

A hidden thought
Repeated, repeated
Focused lens,
Mirror in the dark,
Belt-high photograph.

A deliberate risk
Walking into danger

Alone, always alone,
Accountability avoidance,
Arms-length relationship.

A literary device:
Dime-a-dozen cover-up,
Dunsinane Hill overthrow
Lenina's trigger, and
Heman the Ezrahite's song.

An admission of inability,
Next-best-idea healing
And pain-for-pain revenge
Dissolving under bitter tongue
Beneath a careless sky.

A daily reality
Without memory of time,
Life-in-a-cave echo
Institutionalized blanket
Of threadbare insecurity.

And wanting to live?
. . . Dangerous.

Cold

It is the piercing quality of the cold,
The way my breath is   taken   from [me],
The sudden t o r p   o   r   of
time. It is as though all the   pain   [I've] caused
Hits [me] with icy-hot   anguish
And
           threatens to collapse [my] lungs.
Every tear [I] watched roll,
A single avalanche   coursing
Down soft, unadorned cheeks
Has turned to   frost on the window pane
Of [my] Antarctic   heart
As others make desperate
attempts

To try to see in—
              an impossible task
Given the opacity of the glass
Caused by crystalized melancholy
From the former times
As [I]   tore   [my]   world   apart.
It is in   that instant
                [I] know the truth,
Exhaling, [I] see the misty trail
Of fleeting breath   stalk   through the cold,
                [I] disappear after it.

Christopher Wren's Tombstone

. . . And my mind is trapped orbiting
Some distant Green Star
That New Horizons will fly by
Maybe ten years after
Ultima Thule was photographed.
And I think Eveline's mother
Was probably on to something
I should have known,
("*Derevaun Seraun, Derevaun Seraun*"[v])
Since Solomon said the same—
And I keep seeing myself
In the solitary photograph,
Which her father passed over
Casually: "He is in Melbourne now."[vi]
Reminders are everywhere
Like Absalom's Pillar in
The King's Valley, or
The resigned look in my
Daughter's eyes, knowing
That I won't be there again.
"*Lector, si monumentum requiris, circumspice.*"[5]

---

[5] Quote from a dedication for Sir Christopher Wren, hung by his son near his tomb at St. Paul's Cathedral in England. It translates, "If you would seek my monument, look around you."

Forget Me

Forget me.
I'm not worth
Remembering
. . .
Inconsequential:
As history
To modern minds,
As warning signs
To the blind,
As audible voices
To the deaf,
As encouragement
To the dead,
As forgetfulness
To senility,
As civility
To the marginalized,
As ancestry
To orphans,
As humility
To the deified,
As regulations
To opiates,
As compassion
For the vilified,
As apologies
For the wrongs I've done,

Inconsequential . . .
Forget me.

Black Holes

Black holes
Generate
Magnetic fields
So strong
They tear matter apart,
Down to base elements
Like words
Levied against
The defenseless
r
The furnace
Smelting
The souls
Of those
Sucked
Into the void
Of space
And dangling
At the end
Of filament
Strung
Between two
Poles, awaiting
Electric current
To pass through;
The conduit
Of what will

Kill them.

The tearing
Doesn't stop
At base elements,
But continues
To the trichotomy
Of atoms
Ripping to pieces
The universal fabric
Like a young lion
Among Israel's
Flocks of sheep
Or
Joel's prophecy
About rending
Hearts, not garments
Or
The division
Of soul
And spirit
And human frailty
Anonymously penned
To fearful men
Who prefer retreat
To suffering
And dismiss witness.

Jettisoned
Toward the maw

    By my own hand,
    I can feel
    The gravitational grip
    Constituent parts,
    Exploding
    Dark matter
    Embrace
    Of unseen action
    And merciful pull,
    Keeping the universe
    In order:

Destroying	[my] Collapsed star
The darkness	Imploded
Rending	Corporeality
Light's opposite	Trapped in
A good god	Event horizon
Envisioned	For progress and pain
As the closest	Inexhaustible distance
I can come	While soaring
In describing the	Unbreakable
Hand in which	Stripped down
I have fallen	Trichotomized

    For Christ's sake

Hemingway, Neruda, Chopin, and the Baptist

Self-imposed exile
In the back row
Of my former life,
I remember hearing that
The sun also rises, but
I know it must first set.
Pablo Neruda once said,
"The only thing of danger
Here . . . is poetry,"[vii]
But that was post-Canto.
I can hear the funeral march
Echoing in mental caverns,
But I can't bring myself
To stand up.
I should be compared
To children sitting
In the marketplace
Calling to their playmates
About flutes and dirges,
Because camel hair,
Locusts, and wild honey
Might be fitting
If I wasn't offended
By the cost of things.

Something Less Than What We Are

For Zane Fishel

If you go west fast enough
You can outrun the ever-setting sun,
The universe is a spinning plate
God keeps balanced on a spindle,
Fires kindled and fires fanned
To burn, and burn, and burn the west
To ashes, blowing, whirling on the ground.

Fires rage

Human fires burning
Out the best of us, reducing us
To something less than what we are
And the universe, unmoved, spins on.

Grey, heavy cinders drift in circles
Down upon the heads of the living
Down upon the roads and streets
Down upon your intentions
And down upon my peace

You are Ecclesiastes once read
Before the ardor wanes:

(Yet still one day away!)
The sleepers to their beds,
The mourners to their dead,
While one rises at the chirp
The bird makes in its haste
Searching the smoldering ground
For that sumptuous feast of promise.

   [A friend at least, to hurry along with
   A friend to bear the load of loss
   The sunset turns to Copper in the sky
   Sneaking off to visit Todd beneath the trees
   A forbidden meeting yet a vital end]

The heart quakes in sadness
At the mere mention of it,
The drifting, as a boat unmoored
Loses ground to the tidal sea
On the western edge of the horizon
Awash with heat and pain
Eclipse in wasteland shadows
Of a spinning universe,
Where people are refined.

On Attending a Writing Workshop

There is a certain bondage,
A certain heaviness in living.
Don't get me wrong,
Life is beautiful and worth fighting for.
I've campaigned in dark places of the world;
I've battled on knees stained with
Blood and vomit and tears . . . Wars
Fought hard for those who have hardly fought,
Because I believe their lives are precious;
They matter, and Christ . . .
I have no place in this world.
Would, that times of refreshing would come!
The bondage in living is that I am alive,
Bound to the flesh of this world,
Bound inextricably to a knowledge
That we're not all getting out alive,
Bound to my doubt
That my life will be of any account,
Bound to the darkness of vexing knowledge
Stretched between the posts of shame and anger,
While words lacerate my exposed, transparent skin.
Bound by a desire to protect people
From the consequences of other people's choices…
And bound to fail.
Would, that times of refreshing would come!
The heaviness in living is the weight
Of insurmountable expectations

Placed upon me by I'm not sure who.
The weight of other people's sin,
No, desire for sin,
The weight of bearing with those
Who ask for advice but don't take it,
Who plead for prayer, but hate conviction,
Who want truth, but prefer lies.
The heaviness is the black opaqueness
Of suffocating helplessness as the people
I love so much finger the triggers
Of their next-to-last destructive choice.
Sometimes, I feel there's not much fight
Left in this dog, and I hate euthanasia.
Truth be told, the fist-sized muscle
In my chest is clenched in a defensive posture
Because if I don't,
If I don't,
If I don't constrict
The warm flow of compassion,
If I don't bury
Empathy in a shallow grave,
The burden and bondage
That threaten to overwhelm me
Might just become the millstone.
Christ, I have failed!
I will fail everyone I love.
Would, that times of refreshing would come!
Is there still a hope to live for?
I want there to be.
I want it for everyone else,

So why not for me?
Is there enough space
To spill my blood?
Can I disclose my palpitations here?
Damned if I know,
But doubly if I don't try.
I'll wipe the sweat from my face
And the blood from my wounds.
I'll get up from my knees
In the strength You provide.
My heart reminded me
We have to keep fighting.
If I die, let me die
With a sword in my hand and tears in my eyes!
I'll keep writing.

On Attending a Writing Workshop Redux

▇▇▇ a certain bondage,
A certain heaviness ▇▇▇

Life is
▇▇▇ dark places ▇▇▇

Blood and vomit and tears ▇▇▇

▇▇▇ Christ . . .
I have no place in this world.
Would, that times of refreshing would come!
The bondage ▇▇▇ is ▇▇▇
▇▇▇ the flesh of this world,
▇▇▇ a knowledge
That we're not all getting out alive,
▇▇▇ my doubt
That my life will be of any account,

▇▇▇

Would, that times of refreshing would come!
The heaviness ▇▇▇ is ▇▇▇
▇▇▇ insurmountable expectations

The

desire for sin

—black
—suffocating helplessness as people
I love so much finger the triggers
Of their next-to-last destructive choice.
there's not much fight
Left in this dog, and I hate euthanasia.
the fist-sized muscle
In my chest is clenched
Because if I don't,
If I don't,
If I don't constrict
The warm flow—
If I don't bury

—me

Christ, I have failed!
I will fail everyone I love.
Would, that times of refreshing would come!
Is there still a hope to live for?
I want there to be.
I want it for everyone else,

So why not for me?
Is there ▬▬▬ space
To spill my blood?
▬▬▬▬▬▬▬▬▬▬

Damned if I know,
But doubly if I don't try.
▬▬▬▬▬▬▬▬

My heart reminded me
We have to keep fighting.
If I die, let me die
▬▬▬▬▬▬▬▬▬▬

I'll keep writing.

Struggle

1
"I will not curse, or curse you, God!
My hand is ever to the plow,
But the fallow ground is hard to drive,
And the furrowed land is light, and dry
Stirrings of the wind pass by
Leaving the clods more undefined,
And Job's wife is a distant thought
To curse the life that blood has bought
The lust of heart and flesh and eye
Going back seems less adverse to me."

2
"Ocean waves surge and toss
White-capped whispers stroll across
The shoreline of unsteady minds
Which care, but only inasmuch
As shallow waters stay the norm
And no one questions, no one warns.
Two promontories in the sea:
One is you, the other, me."

1
"Will the roaring water wear away
The firm foundation of our quay?
Will the lee we form survive?
Will the ships port in the bay?

Is the plowed up land enough?"

2
"The way is hard, the going rough,
And scattered seeds don't seem to root
When crows swoop down from roost to rook.
Torrents of the sea descend
And creatures underneath defend
With a fierceness and a guile
Intent on the destruction planned
Before some intervening hand."

1
"And here my questions condescend:
Will the hope of anchor hold?
Will the rain of promise fall?
Will the assumed sun arise?
Will truth and conviction die?
We're not sailors on the oar,
We're not farmers, satchels, seeds,
Can no more endure than a rock
Endures time and tide unchanged."

2
"Yet changes that the swells produce
The holes and pockmarks of abuse
Relentless foaming of the sea
Service us (after a fashion), creatively.
For discipline we must endure
And our example stands on shore."

1
"A sandcastle for all to see, till
Tide rolls in and skimming swirl
Collapses the parapet so formed,
The banners and the spires fall,
The glassy kingdom crumbles down.
The alpha and omega signs
That once upon the flags did fly
Are cast into indifferent tide
Born away to distant shores
Where a different world still looks the same.

[Later that day]
1 [alone]
"I'm riding on a carousel,
The people and the scene all change,
Round and round and up and down,
My horse and I are both the same.
Discouraged farmers still must plant,
And weary seafarers unfurl their sails,
And children build sandcastles despite
What churning waters soon erase
And promontories soaked by tears
Cast upon them, carelessly.
Will endure the crushing surf despite
The way it makes their faces change.
I will not curse you, oh my God!
Despite the wind, despite the clods
Only allow me grace to heed

The correction Job received.
I want the up-and-down to cease
And circular motion terminus!
The horse which never let me down
Has made me sick while on its course,
I'm dizzy from the scenery,
My eyes can't handle any more.
All knowledge and vexation grow,
Together wisdom and sorrow flow,
Waters lap upon my shore
Where other people's boats are moored,
Unless their anchors go behind
The torn veil to the cornerstone,
Their ships will drift out to the deep
While I weep, while I weep!
Their sails are torn, their tillers worn.
Is there hope of safe return,
Or has the Albatross become
A millstone dragging them to drown?
Will the covered seeds yield fruit
Buried in dry tracts of earth?
Can rain clouds hover overhead?
Will the farmer eat unleavened bread?
My hand is still upon the plow,
My horse still moving up and down,
My questions linger in my heart,
My choice is still to wash myself
In the salt of crashing waves, that coat
The shoreline of my unsteady mind
With foaming thoughts and seaweed

Tideline, evidence of what had been.
Sandcastles will again be built
With a hopeful expectation they
May bless someone by existing
Just before they're washed away
Believing that, despite the chance
Of rock or thorn or enemy
The seeds the Faithful Farmer sows
May yet produce a crop.
I'll gladly eat unleavened bread
Beneath the broom tree where I lie,
Where, once, I could only hope to die,
Or leave the safety of the bay
Before my thoughts beget decay
And bless the rocks that mark the way,
My face dressed with eternity."

A Prayer: Part III

Prayer is sound
Emitted from a silent mouth,
Teeth clenched,
Eyes clenched,
Heart clenched,
Juxtaposition:
Graveyard, rolled-away stone,
Wither, ascend,
Buried seed, crop yield,
Hair-cut-off, vow fulfilled,
Wilderness voice,
Parched throat cry: "A Sail!"
Horizon display,
Horizontal relationships,
Vertical ramifications;
Unbridled freedom
And exhaled ambivalence,
Confident expectation
Reliably cast upon the waters
Flowing from the throne:
Ankle-deep trickle,
(cast feathers)
Knee-deep flow,
(cast stones)
Waist-deep current,
(cast bread)
Chest deep torrent,

(cast headlong)
Impossible crossing;
Fruit tree shoreline,
Fishing net cast into
Deep Dead Sea,
Alive! Teeming!
Parted waters, dry land,
Rocks of remembrance,
Twelve stone heart altar,
Dug trench, water-logged sacrifice,
Lowing heifer life consumed,
Down-draft flame
Of Carmel fame,
Little cloud rising
From a drought-filled sea;
Structurally reliable
Gopher wood hull,
Pitch-coated, pinioned wing,
Gold and silver hiding place
In the midst,
Crooked and twisted
Generational crown,
Thorns ignominiously worn,
Thin-lipped moan,
Auto-Rickshaw ride
Down third-world street,
Marketplace acquisition
Of the milk and the meat,
Flesh pot longing laid to rest,
Carried near the priestly breast,

Golden ephod's hidden pocket
Urim and Thumim confidence
Abiding in a golden vest,
Bought without money
And without price;
Structure framed Acacia wood,
Royal-clad Tabernacle,
Seven times blood flicked,
Propitiation at the mercy seat
Of perseverance, character, and hope;
Unashamed, unbridled, unmitigated,
Soul laid bare in security,
Gruesome cargo
And barely muttered sincerity,
Fluttering mantle uncertainly donned,
Twice-struck Jordan parted,
Twice-struck rock prevented,
Quake-triggered avalanche, upheld
By doubting Thomas fingers
On a withered hand,
Outstretched on command,
Staunched bloodflow,
Darkness and a torn veil
Too deep for words
Release . . . at last.

The Scribe and the Prophet

first published in "Pain and Renewal" by Vita Brevis Press

You have read about the sunrise,
Colours of red and pink and gold
Shaded on the bellies of clouds,
Shining amber rays of light
Peaking above the iron hills:
"Earth has not anything to show more fair"[viii]
"Kissing with golden face the meadows green"[ix]
"Thy beams, so reverend and strong"[x]
"An aimless smile that hovers in the air."[xi]

But have you awakened with the dawn,
Offered the sacrifice of eyes-wide-open,
Felt the soft warmth of bursting strand,
Observed the clamour of crimson battle,
Experienced the hope of dark deferred,
Or enjoyed the splendor of the King
Returning to the earth again?
Have you experienced the breaking light
Which causes you to live another day?

Beyond Beersheba

I've traveled at least
    One day's journey
        Beyond failure
Where I left part
    Of myself behind,
I've come far enough,
    It's time for me to die.
I thought I was the broom tree
    In the desert
Under which Elijah lay,
    But I'm no better
Than my fathers,
And
    It's time for me to die.
I will close my eyes
    And sleep
In hope that they
Will never see another day.
    Worthiness is a word
        To cover other people's shame
And grace a misplaced
Bandage for self-inflicted pain.

I am afraid of what I am,
    And I am afraid to face
        All that I am not.
    I am a dead raven,

I am dry Cherith,
    I am the un-resurrected
        Widow's son all the same.

Where is the fire, God?
              You answered once

Afterward:

1 Kings 19:1-8—"Ahab told Jezebel all that Elijah had done, and how he had killed all the prophets with the sword. Then Jezebel sent a messenger to Elijah, saying, 'So may the gods do to me and more also, if I do not make your life as the life of one of them by this time tomorrow.' Then he was afraid, and he arose and ran for his life and came to Beersheba, which belongs to Judah, and left his servant there."

"But he himself went a day's journey into the wilderness and came and sat down under a broom tree. And he asked that he might die, saying, 'It is enough; now, O Lord, take away my life, for I am no better than my fathers.' And he lay down and slept under a broom tree. And behold, an angel touched him and said to him, 'Arise and eat.' And he looked, and behold, there was at his head a cake baked on hot stones and a jar of water. And he ate and drank and lay down again. And the angel of the Lord came again a second time and touched him and said, 'Arise and eat, for the journey is too great for you.' And he arose and ate and drank, and went in the strength of that food forty days and forty nights to Horeb, the mount of God."

The broom tree may be identified as a place of hope, provision, providence, sustenance, growth, faith, and calling. The broom tree may also be identified as a place of fear, doubt, despair, depression, anxiety, hiding, running, failure, uncertainty, loneliness, suffering, loss, struggle, and even confrontation. The broom tree may be some or most or all or one or a few or none of these things. For Elijah, it was the collision of them all. The broom tree was the end, and also the beginning. It was both burial plot and birth place, both failure and freedom. It was a place of getting beyond the self-image, beyond the projection. It was a place of nakedness, a place of surrender, a place of examining actions, weighing frailty; a place where Elijah weighed himself on the scales of God and found himself wanting.

The broom tree is a place I am, a place I thought I was, a place I hate, a place I love, a place I wish I never had to come to and a place I don't wish to leave. Where will you find shade in the desert?

Benediction

To my wife and kids: Thank you for giving me the time and space I needed over the long months to work on this project. Thanks for loving me through.

To my wife: Thank you for reading every poem, for wanting to read every poem, for wanting to listen to my overlong, overwrought explanations about every little detail no one will ever get or know about, for quietly chuckling as I agonized over some minutiae or another, for kissing my face in the place I like best.

To my friends and family who read an early draft when I had other ideas and wrote me poems of solidarity; to Zane, Chris, Tyler, and Geoffrey: thank you for bringing balm for my wounds, or if that is too much to say, then thank you for caring through collaboration.

To my copyeditors/readers/friends/brothers who read through the late drafts and helped me hone my words by asking good questions, giving valuable critiques, and calling a spade a spade; to Tyler, Chris, and Gabriel: Thank you for punching me in the face to bloody my lip, for being more excited than I was, for being some pseudo-heretical version of *Footsteps* (I can see where you dragged my half-dead body ["I'm not quite dead"]). I greatly value your friendship.

To Red Flag Press and Vita Brevis Press: Thank you for seeing something in my work, for giving me just enough to make me believe sometimes that I could write.

To Wes: Thanks for writing hope on your hand all those years ago . . . the ink still bleeds through.

To the bands who have no idea who I am because we were never on tour together, but have impacted me especially during this season with their songs; To Comrades, Ghost Atlas, Convictions, Whale Bones, Demon Hunter, Wolves at the Gate, mewithoutYou, Lost in Separation, Stavesacre, Emery, Dead Poetic, Front Porch Step, Death Therapy, For Today, and Oh, Sleeper: Thank you for your way with words and understanding how they can impact people in unexpected ways. Thank you for putting your pain to music.

To my new associates at Untitled: you know what you did.

I am truly grateful for the input, support, and love that I received during this project from the early, dark days and concepts all the way through to the project's culmination. I honestly never had any idea if a single poem would ever be read by more than two or three people (and I still don't!), but somehow you gave me words that encouraged me to keep pursuing, writing, feeling. You have been the bread of angels.

Notes:

---

[i] From "Purdah" by Sylvia Plath
[ii] From "Eloisa to Abelard" by Alexander Pope
[iii] Employee of the White Star Line, at the launch of the Titanic, *May 31, 1911*
[iv] Painting by Salvador Dali
[v] From "Eveline" by James Joyce
[vi] ibid
[vii] Pablo Neruda remark to the Chilean Armed Forces during a search of his house and grounds
[viii] "Composed Upon Westminster Bridge, September 3, 1802" by William Wordsworth
[ix] "Sonnet 33" by William Shakespeare
[x] "The Sun Rising" by John Donne
[xi] "Morning at the Window" by T.S. Eliot

www.ingramcontent.com/pod-product-compliance
Lightning Source LLC
LaVergne TN
LVHW090036080526
838202LV00046B/3847